Notes From A Nomad

poems by

Sarah Dickenson Snyder

Finishing Line Press
Georgetown, Kentucky

Notes From A Nomad

For Ben
with whom I travel

Copyright © 2017 by Sarah Dickenson Snyder
ISBN 978-1-63534-204-8 First Edition
All rights reserved under International and Pan-American Copyright Conventions. No part of this book may be reproduced in any manner whatsoever without written permission from the publisher, except in the case of brief quotations embodied in critical articles and reviews.

ACKNOWLEDGMENTS

Thank you to the magazines where these poems first appeared:

The Pedestal Magazine: "In Rwanda" (previously titled "Go Count the First Seven Stars")
Panorama: The Journal of Intelligent Travel: "Nyamata Genocide Memorial"
Silver Birch Press "IF I" Series: "Notes from a Nomad" (previously titled "If I Rise")
Passager Books: "Learning Meditation in Mussoorie, India" (previously titled "Practicing Meditation")
immix magazine: "Morning in the Rwandan Hostel"

or were aired: *Poetry Sunday, WCAI*: "Ecosystems"

or were printed on paraphernalia: *Nevermore* Poetry and Arts Festival, 2016: "Washing By Hand," "Routinization of Charisma," and "Directions to My Muse"

Publisher: Leah Maines

Editor: Christen Kincaid

Cover Art: Sarah Dickenson Snyder

Author Photo: Jenny Moloney Photography

Cover Design: Elizabeth Maines McCleavy

Printed in the USA on acid-free paper.
Order online: www.finishinglinepress.com
        also available on amazon.com

Author inquiries and mail orders:
Finishing Line Press
P. O. Box 1626
Georgetown, Kentucky 40324
U. S. A.

Table of Contents

Part I
The Steep Decline 1
2nd Day in Rwanda 2
In Rwanda 3
Morning in the Rwandan Hostel 4
Nyamata Genocide Memorial 5
Next to the Basketball Court in Rinkwave 6
Sick Student Settles 7
Akagera National Park 8
Washing By Hand 9
Elemental Imbalance 10

Part II
Position Fixing 12
Routinization of Charisma 13
Pedaling Away 14
Notes from a Nomad 15
How to Cross a Street in Hanoi 16
Directions to My Muse 17
Cancellation Policy 18
Ecosystems 19
Learning Meditation in Mussoorie, India 20

Part III
Snapchat 22
Lunar Eclipse 23
Near Natmauk, Myanmar 24
Eleuthera 25
Travelogue 26
Istanbul 27
Mala Mala, South Africa 28
Thin Air, Thin Blood 29
Kampot, Cambodia 30

Part I

The Steep Decline

I could see the lake

  as we walked down—a wedge

    of blue in the waves of green—

      Musegera, where a wooden boat barely above

        the water's edge ferries bikes, baskets of bananas,

          pineapples, and beans, maybe twenty people packed in—

        no one no longer isolated from the market life;

      everyone under the same widened sky—

    heat on the red roads, reddened—

    stoic soil remembering

    and the sun unabashed

      as wretchedness

        unlatched.

2nd Day in Rwanda

I've taken a bus up to the top
of one of the thousand hills
in Rwanda, let off at the entry
gate of the wired fence, walked

down a hard-packed, rutted red
path past make-shift houses
with corrugated metal roofs,
lines of laundry, and a few errant

black goats that I thought were dogs.
I step into their home, three young
men who have allowed me in to hear
their stories. It is an empty, dark

room, same dirt floor as the path
outside. The doorway frames
the light let in. They bring in
a hand-made bench for us to sit.

My eyes adjust as they talk
about their lives here in Gihembe—
a refugee camp they've lived in
for years, leaving behind

violence in the Congo. One, maybe
two sentences about mothers,
fathers, sisters, brothers killed.
They will never return they say.

We were teachers there, one tells me
as a child moves into their shadowed
home. He reaches out his open hand—
we touch in air—a brief sweep of skin.

In Rwanda

*Go count the first seven stars
you see—then come tell me,* his mother said
And off the boy ran into twilight,
tilted his small head back and began,
One. Two…three. Waiting for four more
to reach out of the darkening.
So much is never seen, nor allowed

here: plastic bags—
the wind cannot define itself
in a desperate pile along the side
of a red road. Yellow fever—
too many get swept
away—so few show signs
or symptoms. Brooms. Or is it dirt?

Reeds lashed and tied
to a worn pole—words and dust
pushed into unsayable—
so many mothers dead or missing,
one child found outside a mud house,
counting to seven.
There is no eight.

Morning in the Rwandan Hostel

Out my window hibiscus branches
burst into blooms, palm fronds

full and fringed, and a woman carries
a yellow jug filled at the central spigot—

a heavy load. The slap of her flip flops
slows at my open door. I offer

to carry the jug inside, but she's doing
her job, placing it hard on the cement floor.

She nods in a language
of hand-delivered burdens,

on her arm a scar,
a cracked map of what remains.

Nyamata Genocide Memorial

Piled on the pews—a hideous laundry stacked and stained
    (twenty-two years of blood rust unbreathable),
their bodies vanished. But not their clothes—
    bloodied shirts, gray pants, sagging skirts.
Underground the skulls are shelved—
    and skeletal legs and arms laid out
on hundreds and hundreds of wooden slats.
    I could descend to see the hollow remains
but don't. I walk outside,
    exhale, listen for the longed
familiar—wind, birds, children running home
    from school along the dirt road so near
the church—ten thousand people came
    for protection within sacred walls.
A massacre, not one saved.

Next to the Basketball Court in Rinkwave

Our students are on the court
leading drills, all arms and laughter.
I am standing with their bags

& a box of bananas when a group
of young boys swells, spilling
around me, the bags, and the bananas.

Water? they ask, seeing
bottles tucked in pockets of the backpacks.
Sorry, I say, *those are for my students,*

pointing to the swirl of balls and kids.
Food? Money? they ask, more
words I know. I lift

the box of small, curved fruit
in out-stretched hands,
ignite a wrangled cloud of us.

Sick Student Settled

At least there is a breeze—
no running water, toilet clogged

and reeking. Strong sun, but the air
moves through the screens,

the ripped screens, the ragged
mosquito netting and he's sleeping

in the bed—chest not heaving as it was
before hurling anything that was in his stomach

out. There is a rustle of leaves, a lizard
on the wall, a body quieted.

Akagera National Park

On the right is a baboon,
the guide says, and we swerve

our gaze, our lenses. We are
bumping over rutted roads—

see an elephant with ears like
undulating sheets of leather, while he

munches on a branch, hippos slipping
into a watery edge, becoming islands of eyes,

zebras with skin art not for camouflage
but illusion; who knows where one begins

and another ends—the herd
in a huddle as one.

Washing By Hand

Dirt releases—watch the soaping
water color, ring out what lingers,
and hang in the unwrapped sun.

Elemental Imbalance

One day at the public water station
in the refugee camp, the flow slipped

to a trickle, thinned and choked.
There was nothing. Only naked children,

their young mothers, empty plastic
jugs, and a smell of tiredness—

so much effort for a simple bath, water
to drink. That same day as the indifferent world spun,

someone turned on the shower, let it run and run
to hot, steam starting to bead on the mirror—

stepped into the clean torrent, unaware
of what slips down the drain,

moves through pipes into the earth
promising more.

Part II

Position Fixing

Trees spoke out of the rounded earth,
    white against a dark sky—

a whole pageantry of lines awakening,
    nothing unnoticed in this feathered center.

If only changing a life were as wild
    and bordered, if only

there were a lighthouse, instructions
    according to a plan—

nothing left to wishing on stars
    or spinning planets.

Routinization of Charisma

A bird, a blur—
I love a shadow from the sky—

a cloud darkening the sheen of water,
and how the moon strikes the sun

again. So many signs—
the thing itself forgotten.

Cycling

i.
Unsteady wheels rounding
the church parking lot—
Dad growing smaller.

ii.
Feet clipped into pedals,
moving me through air
as if I will lift in morning mist
with Bernoulli's Principle—
along the White River, a company
of cars washing past. I follow
the white line—a guide
on curves of hard tar,
a painting unfolding.

iii.
A line for words
to spill—raw and real,
unreel a life, unwind,
transcribe a thread
to follow.

Notes From a Nomad

If I rise from the earth
invisibly trussed to a sun
in the ripples of fabric,
unwedged, untangled—
I become a hot air balloon
or a small slice of the moon,
unextinguished in a crowd of stars.

How To Cross a Street in Hanoi

Look for a slight opening.
You must be a leaf

to flow on the surface,
the straight force

of moving water. Just walk.
And they will fill in around you.

The motorcycles, the bicycles,
the relentless roar.

Directions to My Muse

Undo the four screws
on the plastic back

of the transistor radio.
Lift off the square with care.

Let the tiny people blossom
in the cup of your palm.

Hold the music, its weight—
write what you see,

It isn't about writing—
it's about seeing.

Cancellation Policy

The wrinkled grayness of remembering—
      opening a screen door,
           hearing its slap
behind my back,
    walking to the edge
        of the porch and shaking the cloth
of me in invisible wind,
    let the flurry
        drift, unnoticed—
           a tingling
mass of molecules
    in the pageantry
        of time,
traveling in a cocoon
    of fragments,
        landing in a nestled curve
           of the ear
                or breath.

Ecosystems

A googly-eyed rock goby
is a fish that lives

in small pools nestled
in rocks near the breach

of waves—little worlds
contained, protected.

Do they wish to leave
their measured realm

so close to an infinite sea?
Do they know how much

spins outside their boundary?
How much will we never know

about what lives outside of us.
I have been with him

for thirty years—
we swirl—

the two of us
in a hot tub,

untrembling, a billion trillion
specks of light beyond our reach.

Learning Meditation in Mussoorie, India

The swami is all analogy,
a practiced linguist, making meaning
from one language to another,

and there were drawings—
round, moon heads, one stick
for the body, lines for fingers—

branded on a page with waxy colors—
the smallness of the fingers,
five little moons of fingernails.

Water kneels to the mountains,
mountains breathe and hum,
and sun speaks to trees.

I am a crimson sari,
meandering, raveling
away from me.

Part III

Snapchat

He was
        almost unrecognizable

in the photograph
        he sent today—the beard,

the grin on top of another world.
        Even in the layered coats, it was evident

how thin he was—my son now a bearded man
        who climbed three passes to get to the base-camp,

a skirt beneath the highest peak. And he was there—
        wrapped in mountains—so close to a sun.

Lunar Eclipse

Only a moon being miraculous
        and two Japanese friends
on cold Adirondack chairs
        beside me

in the dark. We were
        across the earth in their home
six months ago—
        same moon

in an Asian sky—miso tucked
        in a plastic tub behind clothes,
sliding doors, and silent
        mercy.

Here's what they have given me—
        a paper lantern, a lesson
on simmering mushrooms,
        a pleated fan.

Near Natmauk, Myanmar

In a narrow transport boat
slung on the skin of the Yin River

when a speck of something
lodges in my son's eye. He tries

lifting the top lid over the bottom one.
He tries cupping an outstretched hand

to fill with river water and flush it out.
Nothing works—no release;

the tiny assassin, stinging
and stinging him.

Seven hours until Magway
and a local hospital where the speck

is expelled; then he calls home.
I scroll through images of the Yin River,

the villages he's passed in the photographs he's sent—
and one of his first tattoo—

a peacock, feather fan folded,
settled on his shoulder, that pain forgotten.

Eleuthera

Rattling palm fronds,
murmuring waves, birds

heard in the distance—
nature noise where humans visit,

leaving plastic bags to catch the wind—
kites against the blue, tumble weeds

on the slice of sand. The sea content
to lap the earth, move bits of coral.

Travelogue

At home I wash a film
of detritus from sinks, dust

tables where small bits
settle in, sweep floors,

smooth spines, tuck in
flaps of cloth, and clean.

In Tibet, I'm more
focused on breathing

at fourteen thousand
feet as I lift my legs

up stone steps
listen to words

I do not know, see
how others fill a cup of tea

from a worn thermos, offer
us grapes in a temple—

I don't see dust
on surfaces, just in lines

of sunlight—breathe in
the dust of us.

Istanbul
March, 2015

i.
Our movement through the street
is pathless, a wild sea of infinite
arms and heads and scarves.
Multiply what you're imagining
by at least one thousand
and you might see the scene,
this flooding river heading home
in the evening light.

ii.
On a boat in the Bosphorus
Strait everyone has something
flapping in the water's wind
between Asia and Europe. One
woman, her eyes look pulled to the bank—
leather coat and scarf around her
hair keep her contained, along
with the railing she leans against.
We're moving between worlds,
lives stacked below rooflines—
our borders. Small squares
of windows—their apertures.

iii.
Clustered fleshy jewels encased
in a red grenade—a sun
opening—many chambered.
Each pomegranate seed tasting
of something far away—
planted in the depths
of myths—under
worlds—gems to ingest,
earthbound stories
to tell. To follow,
nearly weightless.

Mala Mala, South Africa

A ragged cave has been ripped
into the side of a dead giraffe—
The lions are sated,

sleeping almost, each one grounded
like a Sphinx. Eight of them
with bloodied mouths,

six of us in an open jeep. All silent,
waiting, no one moving,
only flies to bear.

The gun of the guide lies glinting
on the dashboard. Only he, and only they
so used to death.

Thin Air, Thin Blood

On the hike to Machu Picchu,
    a wad of coca leaves tucks
in my cheek—porters carry almost
    everything and my husband holds
my water bottle—my chromosomes
    slow in this high world. Rain and poncho
are weight with the headache.
    Finally on the fourth morning
as the clouds disperse, release exhales
    a thickness of rocks from another
realm—a holy reckoning on the tip of Inca
    toil. Stones on top of stones—
I touch thin lines between the chunks of rock.
    Cut and polished surfaces
form terraced stacks of puzzled granite,
    no mortar needed for them to hold—
a world capped in steps and sides of stone.
    On the train back to Cusco
along the Urubamba River,
    words unfurl in anger
and we are crumbling,
    no one speaking.
We look out the scratched windows—
    no one touching.

Kampot, Cambodia

The hotel where I stay has floating docks
and bungalows, open air ping-pong tables,
with mangos, dragon fruit, and sliced
watermelon in bowls for breakfast, lunch, & snacks.

From there I hop on any banged and rickety
bike sturdy enough somehow
to endure the bumpy slowness.
I am upright, riding

past store fronts small as sheds
patched with colorful corrugated
metal and filled with food
and people and *Hello!*s—

past two bridges—one small, one big—
to a driveway where I turn. *Hello*, a child says,
my name is Ty. She reaches for my hand,
takes me into her school.

Additional Acknowledgements

With many thanks to those who have read my work and pushed it into better places: Barbara Helfgott Hyett, Arthur Sze, Wendy Drexler, Shana Hill, Julia Tait Dickenson, Anne Douglass, Jen Hamilton, Jess Brennan, Laura Foley, Hal Coughlin, and many others around a table at *PoemWorks*, the Tuckerbox, and the Bread Loaf Writers' Conference.

And with gratitude for the many friends I have met on the road and for those with whom I've traveled.

Sarah Dickenson Snyder has been writing poetry since she knew there was a form with conscious line breaks. Pertinent to her work as a writer, she has been an English teacher for many years, a mother for several, and a participant in poetry workshops. She was selected to be part of the Bread Loaf Writers' Conference and has had poems published recently in *The Comstock Review, Damfino Press, West Trade Review, The Main Street Rag, Passager,* and other journals, reviews, and book anthologies. In May of 2016, she was a 30/30 Poet for Tupelo Press. She has full-length collection of poetry, *The Human Contract*, from Aldrich Press.